16-bit Microprocessors, History and Architecture

Patrick H. Stakem

© 2013, 2022

3rd edition

Number 2 in Computer Architecture series

Introduction

The era of the 16-bit microprocessor began in 1975 with the Texas Instruments TMS9900. Actually, the first 16 bit processor was produced by a Japanese Consortium of Fujitsu, Fuji, and Matsushita.. This was the MN1620. The first 16-bit computer was the Whirlwind, during the time when most everyone else was using 6 bits.

The 16-bit microprocessors were a follow-on to the previous 8 bit chips. They offered not only greater integer word size, but more address range, and faster operation than their predecessors. Generally, they operated with 16-bit data, having 16-bit ALU and registers. They could do double-precision 32-bit integer calculations.

They were later superseded by 32-bit processors, which are now the norm for desktop, server, and embedded systems.

Author

The author built his first personal computer in 1976 or so, a 16-bit TI-9900 design. He previously built an Altair 8800 for work in 1975. He went to the Big Computer Faire in Atlantic City, and saw two guys, both named Steve, from California, with a wooden-cased project that probably wasn't going to go anywhere commercially. His

Aerospace career has revolved around support for space-based microprocessors and computers for NASA since 1971.

Mr. Stakem received a Bachelor's Degree in Electrical Engineering from Carnegie Mellon University, and masters in Physics and Computer Science from the Johns Hopkins University. He followed a career as a NASA support contractor since 1971, working at every NASA Site. He taught for the Graduate Computer Science Department at Loyola University in Maryland, the Whiting School of Engineering of the Johns Hopkins University, and Capitol Technology University.

Pictures are from the author's collection, unless otherwise noted. Many thanks to John Culver of cpushack.com for information, assistance, and pictures. Special thanks to J. Chris Hausler for his review.

Mr. Stakem can be found on Facebook and Linkedin.

Computer Architecture

A *computer* performs arithmetic and logic functions on data, and provides flow of control. The arithmetic functions we would like to have performed are additional, subtraction, multiplication, and division. Actually, as we will see later, if we can subtract, we can do any of these operations. Multiplication can merely be repeated addition. The logical operations on binary data include inversion, AND, OR, Exclusive OR, and derivative functions such as Negated-AND (NAND), Negated-OR (NOR), and Negated-Exclusive OR (NXOR). Actually, for two binary symbols, there are 16 possible functions. Only some of these have names (and are useful). As with the mathematical functions, some can be represented as combinations of others. We'll look at mathematical and logical functions applied to binary data, and how the mathematical functions can be expressed in terms of the logical ones.

The *Von Neuman Architecture* says there is no distinction between the code and the data. This was an observation by John von Neumann of the Institute for Advanced Studies at Princeton University. While consulting for the Moore School of Electrical Engineering at the University of Pennsylvania, von Neumann wrote an incomplete "First Draft of a Report on the EDVAC" (computer). The paper described a computer architecture in which the data and the program are both stored in the computer's memory in the same address space. Before this, it was the custom to have separate code and data storage (the

Harvard architecture), and they were not necessarily the same size or format. Von Neumann observed that the code is also data. Most modern microprocessors are this style. For speed, especially in digital signal processors, designers revert to the older *Harvard* architecture, with separate code and data stores, as this gives a speed-up in accessing from memory. In a Harvard architecture, it is difficult to have self-modifying code, which is a good thing from the debugging standpoint.

The fetch/execute cycle

This section discusses how an instruction gets executed. The basic process is referred to as the *fetch/execute cycle*. First the instruction is fetched from memory, and then the instruction is executed, which can involve the fetching and writing of data items.

Instructions are executed in steps called *machine cycles*. Each machine cycle might take several machine clock times to complete. If the architecture is pipelined, then each machine cycle consists of a stage in the pipeline. At each step, a memory access or an internal operation (ALU operation) is performed. Machine cycles are sequenced by a state machine in the CPU logic, driven by a clock source.

A register called the *program counter* contains the location in memory of the next instruction to be executed. The contents of the program counter get automatically updated as the instruction executes. The address of the next instruction to be executed (not necessarily the next adjacent instruction) is put in the program counter. A *register* is a temporary holding memory for data, and is part of the CPU. At initialization time (boot), the program counter is loaded with the location of the first instruction to be executed. After that, it is simply incremented, unless there is a change in the flow of control, such as a branch or jump. In this case, the target address of the branch or jump is put into the program counter.

The first step of the instruction execution is to fetch the instruction from memory into a special holding location called the *Instruction Register*. At this point, the instruction is decoded, meaning a control unit figures out, from the bit pattern, what the instruction is to do. This control unit implements the *ISA*, the instruction set architecture. Without getting too complicated, we could have a flexible control unit that could execute different ISA's. That's possible, but beyond the scope of our discussion here.

With the instruction decode complete, the machine knows what resources are required for instruction execution. A typical math instruction, for example, would require two data reads from memory, an Arithmetic Logic Unit (ALU) operation, and a data write. The data items might be in registers, or memory. If the instruction stream is regular, we can pipeline the operation. We have stages in the pipeline for instruction fetch, instruction decode, operand(s) read, ALU

9

operation, and operand write. If we have a long string of math operations, at some point, each stage in the pipeline is busy, and an instruction is completed at each clock cycle. But, if a particular instruction requires the result of a previous instruction as an input, the scheme falls apart, and the pipeline *stalls*. This is called a *dependency*, and can be addressed by having the compiler optimizing the code by re-ordering. This doesn't always work. When a change in the flow of control occurs (branch, jump, interrupt), the pipeline has to be *flushed* out and refilled. On the average, the pipeline speeds up the process of executing instructions at the cost of complexity.

A special purpose hardware device, purpose-built, will always be faster than a general purpose device programmed or configured for a specific task. This means that purpose-built hardware is the best, yet least flexible choice. Programmability provides flexibility, and reduces the cost of change. A new approach, provided by *FPGA* technology, gives us the ability to reconfigure the hardware and well as the software.

The ALU

An arithmetic logic unit (ALU) performs arithmetic (add, subtract, compare) and logical operations (AND, OR, XOR, negate) on data. The concept was developed by John von Neumann in 1945, in the development of the EDVAC computer. An example of an ALU is the Texas Instruments 74181, the first complete ALU on a chip. Earlier CPU's required a large circuit board of 100's

10

discrete logic chips, or even multiple boards. The 74181 contains 75 logic gates, and is a 4-bit wide CPU, that can be used in multiple units to expand the ALU to 16 bits wide. It implements 16 mathematical and 16 logical operations on 4-bit data in 22 nanoseconds. Later units implemented in a different technology could accomplish these in 7 nanoseconds. Multiply and divide operations can be synthesized by multiple steps in the control unit. Multiply is implemented with repeated ADD's, and divide by repeated subtracts. Shifts can also be synthesized in the firmware. Computer designs using the 74181 included the Data General NOVA 16-bit minicomputer, circa 1968, the DEC PDP-11, The Xerox Alto, the first computer to support a GUI, and the 32-bit DEC Vax-11/780. An example of an 8-bit ALU is the Texas instruments 74AS888 chip.

The Control Unit

The Control Unit decodes the instructions as they are read from memory, and tells each functional unit of the ALU what to do at each clock cycle. It can be implemented as a state machine. The control unit instantiates the instruction set architecture of the computer. The control unit can be hard-wired to decode each instruction, or it can do this task by table look-up in memory. The hard-wired approach is the fastest, but the look-up alternative provides a flexibility to modify and extend the instruction set, within the limitations of the fixed hardware. The definition of the instructions is contained in a read-only memory as firmware. Some write-able memory can be provided to add new instructions. This technique originated in mainframe computers. As the technology advanced, it became possible to include the control unit on the same silicon as the ALU.

Bit slice

The bit slice approach allows you to use modular units to build a CPU as wide as you need. The usual building block size is 4 bits wide, and you can use, for example, 4 of these to implement a 16-bit machine. The control logic is common to all 4 of the ALU chips. Carry's and borrows must propagated along the ALU of course. Besides the 74181 previously discussed, bit slice units included the AMD Am2900, the National Semiconductor IMP-16, and the Intel 3000. The technique was used in the 1956 EDSAC-2 machine, by the University of Cambridge.

The AMD 2901 was a 4-bit slice machine. It included the ALU and 16 registers. The 2910 was the control processor. The 2903 was a later ALU with hardware multiply.

The microprocessors started out as multi-chip units, because all of the functionality would not fit on a single chip, given the technology of the time. As the technology advanced the processor became a single-chip, monolithic unit. Further down the technology road, memory and I/O functions could be implemented on the chip as well.

A microcontroller is a simple CPU plus some memory and Input-output. The idea is to have a single-chip solution to minimize costs. Microcontrollers are not used as general number crunchers, but in dedicated control applications such as elevators, gas pumps, and cell phones.

16-bit microprocessors

This section presents a history and architecture of 16-bit microprocessors. These were generally derived from the 8-bit microprocessors of the time, and had, obviously, a larger word size, but also addressed more memory, and introduced floating point computation capability. Multiply and divide instructions became common.

Floating point provides a different representation of numbers than integer, trading accuracy for dynamic range. It is an analog to engineering or scientific notation, having a fixed precision mantissa, and a power of the base (2, in this case). Necessarily, different hardware than that used for mathematical operations on integers is required. Early 16-bit processors ran MS-DOS, OS/2, and early versions of the Windows operating system. Some 16-bit monolithic microprocessors were used in established minicomputer architectures, to replace circuit boards with hundreds of components.

Intel 8086 family

This section will discuss the hardware components of a computer, specifically that of the Intel x86 family. Starting in 1978, Intel introduced the 16-bit 8086 as a follow-on to the 8-bit 8080 processor. The family continues today, almost 35 years later. It retains the same basic architecture as the earliest chips, and so constitutes a valid family of devices. The newer devices are 64-bit, and nearly a thousand times faster. The x86 architecture at this point supported 16-bit 2's complement integers.

The 80x86 processor family began with the 8086 and 8088 models in 1978 and 1979. The architecture was extended to the 80286 in 1982. Each of these had an associated floating point co-processor, the 8087 and 80287. The architecture was further extended from 16-bits to 32 with the introduction of the 80386 in 1985, and its associated co-processor, the 80387. The 80486 in 1989 combined the co-processor and the main processor on the same chip. In addition, many other companies (such as AMD, NEC, IDT, Texas Instruments, IBM, OKI, Fujitsu, Siemens, and others) also produced these x86 chips and variations under license. The commonality was the ISA-86, the instruction set architecture. The Instruction Set Architecture (ISA) defines the data types, the instructions, the internal architecture of the CPU, addressing modes, interrupt handling, and input/output. The ISA is defined before implementation of the hardware.

The 8088 was the 8-bit external bus version of the 8086. Each memory word took two accesses. This was to save cost on the memory architecture. The 8088 was chosen by IBM to be the basis of their PC architecture. Embedded control versions of the architecture were introduced as the 80188 and 80186. These included some additional devices on the same chip, to reduce chip count in a system, while maintaining compatibility with the ISA-86. The 8088 was initially slower than the Z-80 in many applications, due to the need to access 16-bits in two steps. The 8088 had a 4-byte instruction queue, where the 8086 had a 6-byte queue. This was one way to identify what processor your code was running on.

The 8086 was introduced in 1978 as a true 16-bit processor, with fourteen 16-bit registers, 4 general purpose, 4 pointer/index, 4 segment, the program counter, and the flags register. It could address 1 megabyte of memory using a 200bit address. There were 64k 8-bit I/O ports. The 8086 had 135 basic instructions, including integer multiply and divide, and operated on 8-, 16-, and 32-bit words. 4-bit BCD words were also supported. Instruction length varied from 1-6 bytes. The x86 ISA, common among all the processor models, did not include an illegal instruction trap. There was a non-maskable interrupt, and the interrupts mechanism was essentially the same as for the 8080 8-bit CPU.

The same code would execute on an 8088 and an 8086. If they both had the same clock speed, the 8086 would be faster, because of its wider path to memory. NEC's V-20 product was interesting. It was a direct plug-in replacement for the 8088, but also had an 8-bit Intel 8080 processor compatibility mode. The V-30 chip did the same for an 8086. These devices were designed to ease the transition from 8-bit to 16-bit, by allowing legacy code to still run.

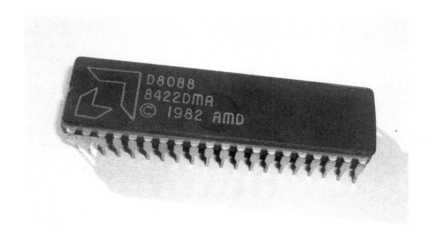

The x86 does not have a flat directly addressed space like most processors. It was a complicated scheme, compared to the flat address space of the later Motorola 68000.

The x86 processor could address 1,048,576 bytes of memory and required 20 address lines in real mode. The internal registers of the processor were 16-bits wide and could only generate 64k different addresses. The designers of the x86 architecture decided to have each 64k segment start on a paragraph address. A paragraph address is always a multiple of 16.

The 4 lower bits of the paragraph address are always 0; therefore, the paragraph address can be expressed as a sixteen bit binary number with the 4 lower bits implied. The paragraph address of the 64k segment is stored in a segment base register.

The 8086/88 had four segment base registers called the code segment (CS), data segment (DS), extra segment

18

(ES), and the stack segment (SS). When an instruction references memory, the paragraph address (shifted left by 4 bits) of the proper segment is added to 16-bit address provided by the instruction. The result is the 20 bit address in the physical memory. The 16-bit address, provided by the instruction, is called the OFFSET within the segment or the effective address.

Recall that there are four segment registers in the x86 architecture, with default assumptions as to which segments they are pointing to.

The CS or code segment register points to the area where instructions to be executed are stored. The IP or instruction pointer contains the offset address within the code segment of the instruction to be executed next. The DS or data segment points to the area where data references will be made. The DS is also used to specify the source for string manipulation instructions. The offset address is provided by the instruction. The SS or stack segment points to the area where the stack will be placed. The offset is provided by the Stack Pointer. The ES or extra segment may be used for data, or destination operands of string manipulation operations. In the 386 and subsequent, there are also the FS and GS segment registers.

Code addressing is simple. The CS register points to the code segment, and the Instruction Pointer (or, Program Counter) provided by the hardware provides the offset. Only a direct address is used. This will be the address of the next instruction to be executed, as automatically calculated by the hardware. Since the instructions are variable length, we need the calculation.

Data addressing is more complicated. An instruction usually specifies a source and a destination. These can be registers or memory or the stack. In different modes of addressing the address is known (or, resolved) at different times. Some of the modes are complicated, and little used. They can simplify the addressing of complex data structures, such as multiple-dimension arrays. The 80286 was an improved model of the 8086. It went on to form the basis of IBM's AT architecture. It had 16-bit wide data, and a 24-bit address. It could operate as a faster 8086, with the old 1 megabyte (20 bit address) limits, or in a native mode, with a 16-megabyte address limit.

There were two queues for instruction pipelining. The pre-fetch queue was an 8-byte look-ahead from the instruction pointer. The decoded instruction queue contained microcode. The 80286 provided virtual memory support and support for multitasking. It carried over the segmented memory architecture of the 8086, where a segment was 64 kbytes in size.

The 8086 reset

A reset causes a special interrupt to the processor.
Several registers are set to particular values:

IP = 0000h ; instruction pointer
CS = FFFFh ; Code Segment register

DS = ES = SS = 0000h   ; data, extra, and stack
segment registers.

After reset on the 8086, the processor accesses an address 16 bytes below the top of memory, fetches the instruction from there, and executes it.

What is 16 bytes below the top of memory? Well, that's the key question. The Operating System, specifically the BIOS, is responsible for putting a proper value there. Since the address is only 16 bytes below the top of memory, we can't put much of a program there, but we can put a Jump instruction to anywhere else in memory.

So, what's there? Again, the Operating System is responsible for putting a program there that does whatever we want to do after a RESET. Do a clean-up, restart a program, etc. If there isn't something valid in those locations, the process still continues, but the results may be less than desirable.

The x86 architecture had a series of co-processors, optimized to specific tasks. The most common example was the floating point co-processors. A co-processor architecture allows concurrent execution with a main processor, executing form the same instruction scheme. This might require a dma-like memory cycle steal mechanism. Synchronism is required between the main CPU and the co-processor(s). Generally, the main CPU has the responsibility for enforcing synchronization. The co-processor generally does not fetch its own instructions; this is the role of the main CPU. The co-processors do fetch their own data.

For a while, the 80286 was actually faster at executing instructions than the follow-on 32-bit 80386 (at the same clock rate), but this advantage was rapidly overtaken by increasing clock rates.

The 8089 intelligent I/O co-processor had two independent channels of 2-cycles DMA, and was capable of program execution, with an instruction set of 53 elements and 19 registers. It was similar in concept to the Channel Controllers for IBM mainframes, which offloaded I/O tasks from the main CPU.

There were two configurations possible with the 8089. In local configuration, the 8089 was on the same local bus as the 8086, and shared with the CPU. In remote mode, it had its own local bus, and a shared system bus with the CPU. Communication with the main CPU was through shared memory. There were handshaking signals for startup and interrupts. DMA, with a 5MHz clock proceeded at 1.25 megabytes per second. The 8089 could function as an intelligent hard disk controller. The chip required its own ROM, RAM, and I/O. The bus interface was the same as for the 8086. It had its own unique instruction set, which was oriented to I/O operations. The unique XFER instruction was, in effect, a DMA transfer. The 8089 could interrupt the main CPU. It made use of control blocks in memory, written by the main CPU.

Since the 8089 read from a device, stored the data, then transferred it to the main CPU, it could also operate on the data as it passed by. It could do byte translations, or table look-ups, but no heavy math.

The 82586 support chip was a local communication controller for 10 Mbps Ethernet. It supported four DMA channels. The 8288 bus controller was used with the 8088 in the IBM pc architecture.

The 80130 was a ROM plus a programmable interrupt controller, several timers, and a baud rate generator. In the ROM was a rudimentary operating system, basically, software in silicon. The firmware contained 35 operating system primitives, including task management, interrupt management, message passing via mailboxes, synchronization, and memory allocation. Tasks had 256 possible priority levels, and 5 possible states, asleep, suspended, asleep/suspended, ready, and running.

80x86 16-bit chips chart

model	company	introduction	data bus	Max word size
8086	Intel	1978	16	16
8087	Intel	1978	16	80
8088	various	1979	8	16
80186	various	1981	16	16
80188	various	1981	8	16
80286	various	1982	16	16
80287	various	1982	16	80
V-20	NEC	1984	8	16
V-30	NEC	1984	16	16

Protected Mode in the 16-bit Intel architecture

Protected Mode was introduced on the 80286 to extend the addressing capabilities of the x86 architecture beyond one megabyte. The 8086 native mode is called REAL mode.

Protected mode on the 80286 is of some academic interest only, because there is no way of returning to real mode, except by a hardware reset. It is referred to by some as virtual mode. The concept was that setup would be done in real mode after reset, and the system would transition to Protected mode for subsequent operations.

Operating systems such as OS/2, UNIX, Linux, bsd, and Windows take advantage of Protected Mode's advanced features. For example, multiple copies of DOS can run under UNIX, sharing system resources transparently.

The 80286 and 80386 enter real mode at reset. This mode is comparable with 8086. By software, you can command an entry to protected mode. On the 80286, it isn't easy to get back to real mode via software. On the 80386 and subsequent processors, you could.

In protected mode, you have all the features of real mode, plus virtual addressing, and protection mechanisms for operating system software. Protected Mode also offered advanced features that can be used by operating systems to support multitasking. The physical address space is what you have to work with. The virtual address space is what you pretend to have to work with. The processor does the dynamic mapping between virtual and physical address. This memory management technique is called address translation, and requires additional overhead on each memory access. On 80286, physical address is $2^{24} = 16$ Megabytes, and the virtual address is $2^{30} = 1$ gigabyte.

80186/188

The 80186 was an embedded version of the 8086, incorporating an integral clock generator, dual dma channels, interrupt controllers, and chip selects. This greatly reduced the number of external chips required in a design. It could address 64k of 8-bit I/O ports, or 32k of 16-bit ports, and supported 256 vectored interrupts. The 186 had roughly twice the performance of the 8086. The 80188 was a 80186, with an 8-bit external bus. This allows for the use of less expensive 8-bit wide memory, at the cost of time. Each memory word access (16-bits) required two 8-bit wide sequential memory accesses.

The NEC V20 was a pin-compatible version of the Intel 8088. It had a software-transparent hardware multiplier, as opposed to the 8088's microcode version. Implemented in CMOS technology, it used much less power. In addition, the V-20 had an 8080 8-bit emulation mode. There were microcontroller versions as well, with timers, parallel ports, and serial ports. The V-30 was the pin-compatible variation of the 8086. A single chip pc was built from the V20 core architecture, with interrupt controller, dma support, timers, art, and clock.

Photo courtesy cpushack.com

8096/80196 (MCS-96)

The Intel MCS-96 family of embedded microcontrollers was derived from the 8061 chip. That chip resulted from a project for the Ford Motor Company, for a 16-bit engine controller. This unit was called the EEC-IV. The 8061 had 8 pulse measuring inputs, 10 pulse generating outputs, and multichannel 10-bit A/D.

The 809x parts operated at 12 MHz. They included a CPU and a 4-channel, 10-bit A/D, and 8-bit PWM, a watch-dog timer, and four general 16-bit timers. They featured hardware multiply and divide, and 8 kbytes of ROM. The 8095 version came with no internal ROM, but did include high speed I/O plus a serial port. CMOS versions of the chip were available. A later model was the 80196.

80386SX

The 80386 was a 32-bit processor, and one of the versions, the 80386sx, had a 32-bit ALU, 32-bit internal data paths, but 16-bit external bus. We mention it here to exclude it from the 16-bit category.

Photo courtesy cpushack.com

Western Digital MCP-1600

This chipset was used in the DEC PDP_11, among others. It had a 3.3 Megahertz clock. The 1611 was the register and ALU chip, the 1621 was the control chip, and the 1631 was the microcode rom chip. It was actually an 8-bit architecture, that could emulate a 16-bit device. Clones of the -11 and -21 were produced by the Soviet Union as the KR581K1 and -K2.

IMP-16

This Western Digital chip was used in DEC's LSI-11. It was a multi-chip design, using a bit slice approach. There was one control ROM, and four 4-bit ALU's. The processor had four 16-bit accumulators. Two of these could be used as Index registers. Follow-on single-chip products included the National Semiconductor PACE and INS8900.

Photo courtesy cpushack.com

The PACE (Processing and Control Element) was a single chip 16-bit processor. It's heritage was the IMP-16 and the Data General Nova minicomputer. The follow-on INS8900 implemented the design in NMOS technology. The PACE had 45 instructions, all being single word. It supported four general purpose accumulators, and six vectored interrupts. Besides the CPU, the chip contained 16 kbytes of RM, timers, and I/O ports. It also featured a 10-word stack, but did not have a multiply or divide instruction.

Z-8000

The Zilog Z-8000 was introduced in 1979. It had sixteen 16-bit registers, that could be used a 8-, 16-, 32- or 64 bit words. Register 15 was the stack pointer. The chip had user and supervisor modes. No compatibility with the earlier 8-bit Z-80 was maintained. The Z-8000 did have built-in dram refresh.

A line of communication controllers, the Z16Cxx, use the Z-8000 core architecture. The Z-8000 found a home in many low-cost Unix boxes in the 1980's. Embedded applications of the Z-8000 included lottery ticket sales machines. The Z-8000 never reached the sales levels of the rival Intel 8086 and Motorola 68000.

Ricoh 5A22

The Richo 5A22 was developed for the Super Nintendo Entertainment System. It was an 8/16 bit processor. It was based on a Western Digital chip developed for Apple. It used the MOS Technology 6502 instruction, extended. It could do multiplication and division.

TMS-9900

Texas Instruments introduced the 9900 chip in 1976. It was a chip version of Texas Instrument's 990 minicomputer. It had 16-bit words, but a 15-bit address bus. There were only three internal registers, but it used the concept of a workspace, where the general purpose registers were kept in memory. The WP register pointed to this workspace. This speeded up context switches, since only the value in the WP register needed to be changed. All illegal (undefined) op codes automatically executed as a NOP, which cannot be said for most processors of the time. The 9900 also had an Execute instruction. (the author fondly remembers the TI-9900 chip, as it was the basis of the first microprocessor system he personally purchased and built). The 9900 was considered by IBM as a basis for their pc, but the Intel x86 architecture was chosen instead. It had the big endian architecture that IBM used, and the 9900 was little-endian. Ti built their own pc, the TI-99/4. This was not a big success.

The 9980 addressed the problem of the 9900 not having embedded peripherals. Unfortunately, they were 8-bit ports. The 9940 was supposed to be a true 16-bit microcontroller, but it was never finished.

TI MSP430

The TI MPS430 is a low power 16-bit microcontroller. It can run at 25 MHz, but is a static design, so the clock can be slowed for lower power consumption. They are many different configurations of the device, featuring combinations of features including timers, PWM, serial I/O, analog to digital converters, analog comparators, digital to analog conversion, hardware multiply, and DMA. There is no external memory bus, but the newest models have internal flash, loaded via serial port. Internal memory goes up to 256 kbytes of flash, with 16 kbytes of RAM. The device is currently in its 6th generation.

Infineon Technologys

Infineon introduced the 16-bit XE166 family in 2007. They also had the C166 family, released in 1990. This lead to the C167 family, the XC167, the XE2000, and the XE166. The architecture was in use as late as 2017 by the Russians NNET company, in regular and radiationed hardened variants.

Motorola 68000

The Motorola 68000 had 16-bit internal and external data busses, but had eight 32-bit wide registers, and math ops supported 32-bit arithmetic. There were also 7 address registers. The processor was introduced in 1979. It was microcoded, and had 3 internal 16-bit ALU's and a 24-bit program counter. The architecture is big-endian. There are 56 instructions, and the minimum instruction size is 16-bits. The 68008 model was a 68000 with an 8-bit external data path and 20-bit addressing, to take advantage of cheaper memory. The 68000 processor contained some 40,000 transistors. It was not derived from the earlier 6800 8-bit architecture, but could use it's 8-bit peripheral and support chips.

The 68000 architecture is still in production after 30 years, although Motorola is now Freescale Semiconductor. The architecture supports seven levels of interrupt, with level seven being the NMI. The interrupt vector table started at memory address 0.

The 68000 architecture, with its simple addressing scheme, a 16 megabyte non-segmented flat address space, was ideal for the emerging Unix operating system on workstations, and also in early laser printers. The architecture supported two privilege levels, user and supervisor, with separate stack pointers. At the time, it was not unusual for the printer to have more overall processing power than the computer it was connected to. By 1982, the 68000 architecture supported virtual memory with the 68010 model. The 68000 model did not support the co-processor interface. In the 68000, all I/O was memory mapped.

The 68000 was second-sourced by numerous companies, and became available in a cmos version for low power. The original 68000 dissipated around 1.35 watts, while the CMOS version used 0.4 watts at 20 MHz, and the power consumption was reduced with slower clock speeds. Thirty-two bit arithmetic was handled in microcode as a 2-step process. The 68000 was a big chip, with non-multiplexed 24-bit address and 16-bit data lines. The 68008 model had an 8-bit external data bus to use with cheaper memory. The 68010 model increased support for the implementation of virtual memory. The 68012 model had a 30-bit address bus.

Embedded controller models of the 68000 evolved from the basic architecture, and a fully-static core version became available. When idle, this required only 2 microwatts. The 683xx series was the embedded line. 68000's found use in Industrial control as programmable logic controllers (PLC's) from Allen-Bradley, Texas Instruments, and Siemens. The 68k embedded processors are found in video games, telecomm switching equipment, The TI-89 and TI-92 calculators, and others. The 68ECxx embedded core version evolved into the Dragonball processors from Freescale.

The 68200 was Motorola's 32-bit microcontroller, it had the 68000 CPU plus 2k x 16 bit ROM, and 128 x 16 bits RAM. It included dual 16-bit I/O ports, with a second timer-I/O port that added 4 I/O lines. There were three 16-bit timers. The instruction set was a subset of the 68000. There were 15 vectored interrupts, and a synchronous/asynchronous serial communication. The parallel I/O lines could be used to interface to a system bus, and the chip could take the master or helper role. DMA was available. Most instructions took three clock periods. A 16-bit x 16-bit multiply took 21 clocks. The chip was also available in a ROM-less version,

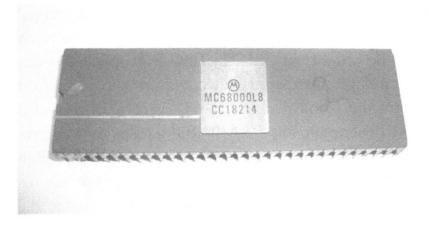

Freescale 68HC16

The Freescale 68HC16 is a 16-bit follow-on to the earlier 8-bit Motorola 68HC11 microcontroller. The Freescale XGATE is a 16-bit RISC processor derived from the same architecture.

DEC LSI-11

The Digital Equipment Corporation LSI-11 was a chip-version of the 16-bit minicomputer architecture of the PDP-11. DEC's first microprocessor, it was introduced in 1975 as a multi-chip set. It was a microcoded device, and the microcode could be used to extend the instruction set.

Floating point operations were supported. It was not quite the same architecture as the standard PDP-11 microcomputer.

The members of the chip set were the Data chip, the Control chip, and one or more MICROM memory chips. The Data chip implemented the instruction execution path of the LSI-11 chip set. The Data chip operated under the control of microwords fetched from the MICROM chips by the Control chip. The Control chip provided address generation for the MICROM chips and control for external data access. The MICROM chip was a high speed 512 x 22 bit ROM which supplied micro-instructions to the Data and Control chips under the direction of the Control chip. Up to four MICROMs were allowed in a system Two of these implemented the base PDP-11 instruction set; a third was required to implement the extended (EIS) and floating (FIS) instruction sets.

1750A

The MIL-STD-1750 lays out a formal definition of a 16-bit instruction set architecture. It does not specify an implementation. The standard allows for memory mapping up to 220 16-bit words. There were 16 general purpose registers. Some can be used as index registers, some as base registers. Any register can be used as the stack pointer. Both 16 and 32-bit integer arithmetic are supported, as well as 32- and 48-bit floating point.

There are many implementations of the 1750A architecture, including several that are built as radiation-hardened pieces. One example is the Fairchild F9450.

Photos courtesy cpushack.com

The preferred language for the 1750A was Jovial, an Algol language variant; later, ADA and c were used as well. The 1750A is found in many aircraft and missile applications by the United States Armed Forces and their allies. A quick list of examples include the USAF F-16 and −18, the AH-64D helicopter, and the F-111. The architecture is also used by the Indian Space Research Organization (ISRO), and the Chinese Aerospace industry. In 1996, the 1750A architecture was declared obsolete for future military projects.

The 1750A found applications in many space projects, including NASA's Earth Observation Satellites (EOS) Aqua, Terra, and Aura. It was used on ESA missions

Cluster and Rosetta. JPL used seven of the processors on the Cassini Mission to Saturn, and more units on Mars Observer and Mars Global Surveyor. It was used on the Clementine spacecraft, a NASA-Naval Research Laboratory Program to study the Moon. The 1750A was deployed on the Johns Hopkins University Applied Physics Laboratory's MSX – Midcourse Space Experiment spacecraft, which used nine. The 1750A flew on EUVE, MSTI -1, -2, & -3, Landsat-7, NEAR, and is on the GOES-13, GOES-O, and GOES–P NOAA spacecraft. The SPOT-4 mission included a F9450, a National Semiconductor implementation. GEC-Plessy also manufactures a radiation-hard RH1750A.

HP BPC

In 1975, HP introduced the BPC, the world's first 16-bit microprocessor, using HP's NMOS-II process. The BPC was usually packaged in a ceramic hybrid module with the EMC and IOC chips, which added extended math and I/O instructions. The hybrid was developed as the heart of the new 9825 desktop computer. The later 9845 workstation added an MMU chip. These were the forerunners of personal computers and technical workstations.

The HP 3000 series was a 16-bit architecture, later extended to 32 bit. These were used in HP minicomputers.

WDC 65816

The Western Digital Design Center developed the 65816 16-bit chip. It was a type of hybrid, with an enhanced 8-bit 6502 architecture, and 16-bit registers. It featured expanded memory addresses to 24 bits. At boot, the chip was essentially a 6502. A two-instruction sequence switched it to 16-bit mode. The design was driven by Apple Computer. The chip was also used by Atari. The 65C816 featured a fully static core, allowing the processor clock to be stopped without the loss of state. The chip was second-sourced by several vendors, and is still available. It is also available as RTL code for Verilog, allowing implementation in an ASIC or FPGA.

Signetics 8x300

The 8x300 was a 16-bit microcontroller. Data could be 1 bit to 8 bits in width. It had eight 8-bit wide registers. Each instruction was executed in one cycle, which is a characteristic of a RISC architecture. Signetics 8x300 parts formed the basis for electronics on Goddard's MMS (Multi-Mission Modular Spacecraft, including SMM, Landsat, and Hubble Space Telescope, and on the Shuttle-attached OSS pallets.

PIC

PIC is a family of Harvard architecture microcontrollers made by Microchip Technology, derived from the PIC1650 originally developed by General Instrument's Microelectronics Division. The name PIC initially referred to "Peripheral Interface Controller".

The PIC architecture is characterized by its multiple attributes, including separate code and data spaces (Harvard architecture) for devices other than PIC32, which has a Von Neumann architecture. It has a small number of fixed length instructions, with most instructions being single cycle execution (2 clock cycles, or 4 clock cycles in 8 bit models), with one delay cycle on branches and skips. There is One accumulator (W0), the use of which (as source operand) is implied (i.e. is not encoded in the opcode), All RAM locations function as registers as both source and/or destination of math and other functions. A hardware stack is used for storing return addresses. A fairly small amount of addressable data space is provided (typically 256 bytes), which can be extended through memory banking. The program counter is mapped into the data space and writable (this is used to implement indirect jumps).

In the PIC18 series, the program memory is addressed in 8-bit increments (bytes), which differs from the instruction width of 16-bits. So they are a type of hybrid 8-bit/16-bit architecture.

The PIC architecture is characterized by its multiple attributes, including separate code and data spaces (Harvard architecture) for devices other than PIC32, which has a Von Neumann architecture. It has a small number of fixed length instructions, with most instructions being single cycle execution (2 clock cycles, or 4 clock cycles in 8 bit models), with one delay cycle on branches and skips.

There was one accumulator (W0), the use of which (as source operand) is implied (i.e. is not encoded in the opcode), All RAM locations function as registers for source and/or destination of math and other functions. A hardware stack is used for storing return addresses. A fairly small amount of addressable data space is provided (typically 256 bytes), which can be extended through memory banking. The program counter is mapped into the data space and writable (this is used to implement indirect jumps).

There is no distinction between memory space and register space because the RAM comprises both memory and registers, and the RAM is usually just referred to as the register file or simply as the registers.

PICs have a set of registers that function as general purpose RAM. Special purpose control registers for on-chip hardware resources are also mapped into the data space. The address-ability of memory varies depending on device series, and all PIC devices have some banking mechanism to extend addressing to additional memory. Later series of devices feature move instructions which can cover the whole addressable space, independent of the selected bank. In earlier devices, any register move had to be achieved via the accumulator.

External data memory is not directly addressable except in some high pin count PIC18 devices. The code space is generally implemented as ROM, EPROM or flash ROM. In general, external code memory is not directly addressable due to the lack of an external memory interface. The exceptions are PIC17 and select high pin count PIC18 devices.

PICs handle (and address) data in 8-bit chunks. However, the unit of address-ability of the code space is not generally the same as the data space. For example, PICs in the baseline and mid-range families have program memory addressable in the same word size as the instruction width, i.e. 12 or 14 bits respectively. In contrast, in the PIC18 series, the program memory is addressed in 8-bit increments (bytes), which differs from the instruction width of 16 bits. This makes them hard to characterize.

PICs have a hardware call stack, which is used to save return addresses. The hardware stack is not software accessible on earlier devices, but this changed with the 18 series devices.

A PIC's instructions vary from about 35 instructions for the low-end PICs to over 80 instructions for the high-end PICs. The instruction set includes instructions to perform a variety of operations on registers directly, the accumulator and a literal constant or the accumulator and a register, as well as for conditional execution, and program branching.

Some operations, such as bit setting and testing, can be performed on any numbered register, but bi-operand arithmetic operations always involve W (the accumulator), writing the result back to either W or the other operand register. To load a constant, it is necessary to load it into the W register before it can be moved into another register. On the older cores, all register moves needed to pass through W, but this changed on the "high end" cores.

PIC cores have skip instructions which are used for conditional execution and branching. The skip instructions are 'skip if bit set' and 'skip if bit not set'. Because cores before PIC18 had only unconditional branch instructions, conditional jumps are implemented by a conditional skip (with the opposite condition) followed by an unconditional branch. Skips are also of utility for conditional execution of any immediate single following instruction.

The architectural decisions are directed at the maximization of speed-to-cost ratio. The PIC architecture was among the first scalar CPU designs and is still among the simplest and cheapest. The Harvard architecture—in which instructions and data come from separate sources—simplifies timing and microcircuit design greatly, and this benefits clock speed, price, and power consumption.

The PIC architectures have small, easy to learn instruction set. They are a RISC architecture. They have a built in oscillator with select-able speeds, and feature in-circuit programming plus in circuit debugging. There is a wide range of I/O interfaces including I^2C, SPI, USB, USART, A/D, programmable compare-ators, PWM, LIN, CAN, PSP, and Ethernet.

The PIC architectures do have several limitations, including only a single accumulator. Register-bank switching is required to access the entire RAM of many devices. Operations and registers are not orthogonal; some instructions can address RAM and/or immediate constants, while others can only use the accumulator.

The hardware call stack is not addressable, so preemptive task switching cannot be implemented. Software-implemented stacks are not efficient, so it is difficult to generate re-entrant code and support local variables.

Rad-hard

Radiation-hardened parts are required for space missions. and for nuclear power plant electronics.

Renesas has a rad-hard 16 bit CMOS processor. It is the HS-80c86RH.

ESA, the European Space Agency, funded the development of a space-rated 16-bit microprocessor in the early 1990's. Built by Dynex Semiconductor, the MA3750 was a multi-chip architecture built in CMOS/SOS technology, capable of 2 million instructions per second (mips) performance.

RTX2010

The Intersil RTX2010 is a radiation-hardened 16-bit processor organized as a stack machine. The architecture supports direct execution of the Forth language. The Forth environment can be seen as a dual-stack virtual machine. The chip has two stacks, each 256 words deep. Context switches only take a single machine cycle. The interrupt latency is 4 cycles, making the processor ideal in real-time applications.

The initial application came in a gate array in 1983, proceeding to a chip implementation by Harris Corporation in 1988.

The RTX2010 was used in numerous NASA missions, including the Advanced Composition Explorer (ACE), the NEAR/Shoemaker mission, Timed, IMAGE (2000), instruments on AXAF, EOS, and EUV, MSX, XTE, Cassini, and MagSat.

Atmel

Atmel has made the SPARC V-7 and V-8 32-bit architecture available in rad-hard versions for 16 years. the TSC695 and AT697F have seen sales of around 3,000. There is an accompanying SpaceWire Remote Terminal Controller. th AT7910E.

Microchip

Microchip has a series of Rad-hard ASIC's. The Multichip wafer can host a series of rad hard architectures.

Floating point co-processors

The floating point co-processor in the Intel architecture executes from the same instruction stream as the main processor. For operand fetch, the co-processor uses a memory cycle steal, something like a DMA operation as far as the main processor is concerned. The co-processor has its own set of internal registers, organized as a stack. Registers are 80 bits wide. Operations include the basic operations of arithmetic, plus trigonometric, logarithmic, and exponential operations.

The Intel numeric co-processors do operations on extended precision integer (64-bit) and floating point format. They are faster than the main processor in these operations, and, in addition, operate in parallel with it. For example, a 64 x 64 bit multiply would takes 2100 microseconds on the 8086, but only 30 microseconds on the 8087 co-processor, a speed up of a factor of seventy. For something like a tangent operation the results are more impressive: 110 microseconds versus 13,000 for the equivalent integer operation. The floating point co-processor allowed for the replacement of software emulations of the calculations on the main integer CPU.

Photo courtesy, cpushack.com

The Intel processors and associated co-processors form a tightly coupled pair. The main processor does all the instruction fetching. In addition, it is responsible for transferring data to the co-processor's registers. Execution of co-processor instructions proceeds in parallel with those of general instructions. The co-processor recognizes its own instructions, and executes them. Co-processor instructions start with a hex F. The main processor ignores co-processor instructions. Between the main CPU and the co-processor, there is a busy/wait handshake mechanism for coordination. There is a control word and a status word in internal registers in the floating point unit. The floating point unit also maintains its own instruction pointer and an operand pointer. The floating point unit can generate exceptions including invalid operation, attempted division by zero, normalized, overflow, underflow, and inexact result.

The instruction set includes load and store; the basic add, subtract, multiply, and divide; compare; square root; and certain pre-calculated constants in floating point format such as zero, one, pi, $\log_2(10)$, and others.

The 8087 and 80287 were floating point co-processors for the 8086 and 80286, respectively.

16-bit 80x86 family pedigree

8086	16-bit processor, circa 1978. addresses 1 megabyte 6-byte instruction queue, 6 MHz
8088	8-bit external bus version of 8086. Chosen by IBM to be the basis for the pc; 4 byte instruction queue
80186	advanced features integrated on-chip
80188	8-bit external bus interface version of 80186
80286	chosen by IBM to be basis of AT machines

16-bit Minicomputers

DEC PDP-11

The DEC PDP-11 was a circa 1970's 16-bit minicomputer built from discrete TTL parts. It was a 16-bit design, and the host for the first UNIX operating system. By 1975, the basic architecture was moved to a single board, multichip design. It used the 4-chip LSI-11 chipset from Western Digital. The PDP-11 influenced the development of the Motorola 68000, the C programming language, the operating systems CP/M and MS-DOS, and many other follow-on activities. Heathkit produced a kit-format personal PDP-11 in 1977, selling for $1300. DEC eventually sold over 170,000 units.

Data General NOVA

The Data General NOVA was a 16-bit microcomputer, built from discrete logic on two 15 inch by 16 inch circuit boards. It was introduced in 1969 for $4,000, but adding 4 kilobytes of 2.25 microsecond access core memory upped the price to $8000. The NOVA went on to sell over 50,000 units. A BASIC interpreter was available on paper tape. The single chip implementation was called the micro-NOVA. The NOVA 4 made the switch from magnetic core memory to DRAM. The NOVA architecture was load-store, with four accumulators. Two could be used as index registers. The ALU was built up from 4-bit 74181 chips. Later models used the AMD 2901 bit slice processor.

AGC

The Apollo Guidance Computer (AGC) was developed by the MIT Instrumentation Lab, headed by Charles Stark Draper, using heritage from the Polaris submarine-launched missile guidance computers. It was a 16-bit design, built by Raytheon. The AGC was critical for guidance and navigation.

There were two Apollo Guidance computers on each mission, one in the Command Module; and one in the

Lunar Lander. This proved to be a good idea on Apollo 13, which suffered an explosion that crippled the Command module on the way to the moon. The computer in the Lunar Lander was re-tasked to provide guidance computations to get the astronauts back to Earth, before the Command Module would be re-activated for re-entry.

Later, the AGC design was used as the basis for aircraft fly-by-wire systems and in a Navy Deep Sea Submersible project.

The calculations were done internally in metric, but the astronauts (mostly test pilots) preferred English units for display.

The computer had a complexity of some 5,000 RTL logic gates from Fairchild Semiconductor (a pc has 100's of millions), which represented some 60% of the total US production of microcircuits at the time. The computer was a 16-bit machine, and had a 1.7 microsecond cycle time (current machines are sub-nano-second). It had 2048 bytes of random access memory, and 36k of read-only memory, both implemented in a magnetic core technology. There were four registers, the accumulator, the program counter, the remainder from the DV instruction or the return address after a transfer of control instruction, and the lower product after a multiply instruction. There were five vectored interrupts.

The guidance computers had 152 kilobytes of storage for the entire mission. The size was 6 inches, x 1 foot x 2 feet; they weighed 70 pounds, and used 55 watts of electricity. They were constructed of 5600 3-input nor gates, and featured a cycle time 11.7 microseconds. The clock was 1.024 MHz.

The Apollo computers were programmed in YUL – an assembly language of 40 operations, and there was an interpretive language for math-intensive calculations. The software was released in January of 1966, with the first flight was in August 1966. The unit was used until 1975. No in-flight errors were ever attributed to software. None. This was after 2,000 person-years of independent verification and validation (IV&V).

Thumb Mode of ARM processor

The Thumb Instructions set are a 16-bit subset of the ARM-7 32-bit architecture. This reduces functionality but provides a greater code density. Sections of code that are computer-intensive can be hand-optimized for the Thumb mode. Most Thumb instructions map directly to ARM opcodes. Thumb mode is supported in most ARM architectures.

The 20-bit CADC

Who knows what else existed in labs and research establishments at the time? Recently, an embedded processor project that predates the Intel 4004 was declassified, a set of 6 custom chips for the fly-by-wire F-14 Tomcat fighter aircraft's Central Air Data Computer (CADC). It was not a complete single-chip design, though. It was developed by Ray Hold, who was finally able to discuss his work for the Navy after 1998. The work was started in 1968. The previous CADC for the F-4 Phantom aircraft was an electro-mechanical device. The design was complete in June of 1970, and flew in December. It was implemented in pmos technology, and met the full mil-spec temperature range. the chips were fabricated by American Microsystems. The design came in at under 75,000 transistors, most of which were in the ROM storage, not the CPU.

The design was totally digital, and dual redundant, with self-checking. Since it interfaced to analog components, there were both A/D and D/A converters. It used 10 watts of power. It's job was to compute and display data for the pilot, and control the targeting and launch of the aircraft's missiles. It also controlled the control surfaces on the plane's wings and tail. It used fixed-point 2's complement arithmetic with 20-bit data. It used a 375 KHz clock, and had parallel multiply and divide units. There were 16 data registers and 128 words of memory. Instructions were held in ROM.

And, in conclusion....

Modern computers started out using relays and vacuum tubes for switching elements. The semiconductor revolution provided diodes for logic functions, and transistors for switching. As the technology allowed for putting multiple transistors and other elements on a single substrate, the integrated circuit began to be widely used. The complexity of the devices increased according to an exponential growth law, the technology feeding upon itself. This allowed for functions such as an arithmetic-logic unit to occupy one chip. Then, at around 4,000 transistors capacity, an entire 4-bit CPU that executed instructions could be implemented. Not much later the 8-bit CPU was developed. Memory and I/O functions also benefited from the increasingly complex solid state-electronics. The next step along the way was the 16-bit processor, then 32 and 64.

Glossary

1's complement – a binary number representation scheme for negative values.

2's complement – another binary number representation scheme for negative values.

2-wire – twisted pair wire channel for full duplex communications. Still needs a common ground.

Accumulator – a register to hold numeric values during and after an operation.

ACM – Association for Computing Machinery; professional organization.

ALU – arithmetic logic unit.

Analog – concerned with continuous values.

AND – logical operation on data. Output is true, if and only if both inputs are true

ANSI – American National Standards Institute

ASCII - American Standard Code for Information Interchange, a 7-bit code; developed for teleprinters.

ASIC – application specific integrated circuit.

Assembly language – low level programming language specific to a particular ISA.

Async – asynchronous; using different clocks.

Baud – symbol rate; may or may not be the same as bit rate.

Baudot – a five-bit code used with teleprinters.

BCD – binary coded decimal. 4-bit entity used to represent 10 different decimal digits; with 6 spare states.

Big-endian – data format with the most significant bit or byte at the lowest address, or transmitted first.

Binary – using base 2 arithmetic for number representation.

BIST – built-in self test.

Bit – smallest unit of digital information; two states.

Blackbox – functional device with inputs and outputs, but no detail on the internal workings.

Boolean – a data type with two values; an operation on these data types; named after George Boole, mid-19th century inventor of Boolean algebra.

Borrow – mathematical operation when a digit become smaller than limit and the deficiency is taken from the next digit to the left. Occurs during subtraction.

Buffer – a temporary holding location for data.

Bug – an error in a program or device.

Bus – data channel, communication pathway for data transfer.

Byte – ordered collection of 8 bits; values from 0-255

Cache – faster and smaller intermediate memory between the processor and main memory.

CADC – Central Air Data Computer

Carry – arithmetic result, when a digit is larger than a limit and the extra is moved to the left.

CAS – column address strobe (in DRAM refreshing)

Chip – integrated circuit component.

Clock – periodic timing signal to control and synchronize operations.

CMOS – complementary metal oxide semiconductor; a technology using both positive and negative semiconductors to achieve low power operation.

Complement – in binary logic, the opposite state.

Control Flow – computer architecture involving directed flow through the program; data dependent paths are allowed.

co-processor – another processor to supplement the operations of the main processor. Used for floating point, video, etc. Usually relies on the main processor for instruction fetch; and control.

Core – early non-volatile memory technology based on ferromagnetic toroids.

Cots – commercial, off-the-shelf.

CPU – central processing unit.

DCE – data communications equipment; interface to the network.

DEMUX – de-multiplex.

Digital – using discrete values for representation of states or numbers.

DMA - direct memory access (to/from memory, for I/O devices).

Double word – two words; if word = 8 bits, double word = 16-bits.

Dram – dynamic random access memory.

Drum memory – obsolete storage media using large cylindrical magnetic media.

DTE – data terminal equipment; communicates with the DCE to get to the network.

DTL – diode-transistor logic

EIA – Electronics Industry Association.

Embedded system – a computer systems with limited human interfaces and performing specific tasks. Usually part of a larger system.

Epitaxial – in semiconductors, have a crystalline overlayer with a well-defined orientation.

Eprom – erasable programmable read-only memory.

EEprom – electrically erasable read-only memory.

Exception – interrupt due to internal events, such as overflow.

Fail-safe – a system designed to do no harm in the event of failure.

FET – field effect transistor.

Fetch/execute cycle – basic operating cycle of a computer; fetch the instruction, execute the instruction.

Firmware – code contained in a non-volatile memory.

Fixed point – computer numeric format with a fixed number of digits or bits, and a fixed radix point Integers.

Flag – a binary indicator.

Flip-flop – a circuit with two stable states; ideal for binary.

Floating point – computer numeric format for real numbers; has significant digits and an exponent.

FPGA – field programmable gate array.

FPU – floating point unit, an ALU for floating point numbers.

Full duplex – communication in both directions simultaneously.

Gate – a circuit to implement a logic function; can have multiple inputs, but a single output.

Half-duplex – communications in two directions, but not simultaneously.

Handshake – co-ordination mechanism.

Harvard architecture – memory storage scheme with separate instructions and data.

Hexadecimal – base 16 number representation.

Hexadecimal point – radix point that separates integer from fractional values of hexadecimal numbers.

HP – Hewlett-Packard Company. Instrumentation and computers.

IEEE – Institute of Electrical and Electronic Engineers. Professional organization and standards body.

IEEE-754 – standard for floating point representation and operations.

Index register – register to hold addresses.

Infinity - the largest number that can be represented in the number system.

Integer – the natural numbers, zero, and the negatives of the natural numbers.

Interrupt – an asynchronous event to signal a need for attention (example: the phone rings).

Interrupt vector – entry in a table pointing to an interrupt service routine; indexed by interrupt number.

I/O – Input-output from the computer to external devices, or a user interface.

IP – intellectual property; also internet protocol.

IP core – IP describing a chip design that can be licensed to be used in an FPGA or ASIC.

ISA – instruction set architecture, the software description of the computer.

ISO – International Standards Organization.

ISR – interrupt service routine, a subroutine that handles a particular interrupt event.

JTAG – Joint Test Action Group; industry group that lead to IEEE 1149.1, Standard Test Access Port and Boundary-Scan Architecture.

Junction – in semiconductors, the boundary interface of the n-type and p-type material.

Kilo – a prefix for 103 or 210

Ladder logic – description of relay-based logic circuits, Obsolete.

Latency – time delay.

Little-endian – data format with the least significant bit or byte at the highest address, or transmitted last.

Logic operation – generally, negate, AND, OR, XOR, and their inverses.

LSB – least significant bit or byte.

Machine language – native code for a particular computer hardware.

Mainframe – a computer you can't lift.

Mantissa – significant digits (as opposed to the exponent) of a floating point value.

Math operation – generally, add, subtract, multiply, divide.

Mega - 10^6 or 2^{20}

Microcode – hardware level data structures to translate machine instructions into sequences of circuit level operations.

Microcontroller – microprocessor with included memory and/or I/O.

Microprocessor – a monolithic CPU on a chip.

Microprogramming – modifying the microcode,

Minicomputer – smaller than a mainframe, larger than a pc.

MIPS – millions of instructions per second; sometimes used as a measure of throughput.

Modem – modulator/demodulator; digital communications interface for analog channels.

MSB – most significant bit or byte.

Multiplex – combining signals on a communication channel by sampling.

Mux - multiplex

NAN – not-a-number; invalid bit pattern.

NAND – negated (or inverse) AND function.

NASA – National Aeronautics and Space Administration.

NDA – non-disclosure agreement; legal agreement protecting IP.

Negate – logical operation on data; changes the state.

Nibble – 4 bits, ½ byte.

NIST – National Institute of Standards and Technology (US), previously, National Bureau of Standards.

NMI – non-maskable interrupt; cannot be ignored by the software.

NOR – negated (or inverse) OR function

Normalized number – in the proper format for floating point representation.

NRE – non-recurring engineering; one-time costs for a project.

Null modem – acting as two modems, wired back to back. Artifact of the RS-232 standard.

NVM – non-volatile memory.

Nxor – logical operation on data; negated XOR.

Nyquist rate – in communications, the minimum sampling rate, equal to twice the highest frequency in the signal.

Octal – base 8 number.

Off-the-shelf – commercially available; not custom.

Opcode – part of a machine language instruction that specifies the operation to be performed.

OR – logical operation on data; output is true if either or both inputs are true.

Overflow - the result of an arithmetic operation exceeds the capacity of the destination.

Paradigm – a pattern or model.

Paradigm shift – a change from one paradigm to another. Disruptive or evolutionary.

Parallel – multiple operations or communication proceeding simultaneously.

Parity – an error detecting mechanism involving an extra check bit in the word.

PC – personal computer, politically correct, program counter.

PCB – printed circuit board.

Pic – a microcontroller from Microchip Technology.

Pinout – mapping of signals to I/O pins of a device.

PLC – Programmable logic controller, embedded device for automation.

PLD– programmable logic device; generic gate-level part that can be programmed for a function.

PROM – programmable read-only memory.

QML - user interface and specification language.

Quad word – four words. If word = 16-bits, quad word is 64 bits.

Queue – first in, first out data buffer structure; hardware of software.

Rad – unit of absorbed radiation dose; 100 ergs per gram; also, radian, angular measurement.

Radix point – separates integer and fractional parts of a real number.

RAM – random access memory; any item can be access in the same time as any other.

RAS – Row address strobe, in dram refresh.

Register – temporary storage location for a data item.

Reset – signal and process that returns the hardware to a known, defined state.

RISC – reduced instruction set computer.

ROM – read only memory.

Real-time – system that responds to events in a predictable, bounded time.

RS-232 – EIA telecommunications standard (1962), serial with handshake.

RTL – register transfer level, description of logic circuit.

SAM – sequential access memory, like a magnetic tape.

Self-modifying code – computer code that modifies itself as it run; hard to debug.

Semiconductor – material with electrical characteristics between conductors and insulators; basis of current technology processor and memory devices.

Semaphore –signaling element among processes.

Serial – bit by bit.

Seu – single event upset; radiation induced upset in a device.

Shift – move one bit position to the left or right in a word.

Sign-magnitude – number representation with a specific sign bit.

Signed number – representation with a value and a numeric sign.

SOC – system on chip.

SOS – Silicon on Sapphire, an inherently radiation tolerant (yet, expensive) fabrication.

Software – set of instructions and data to tell a computer what to do.

SRAM – static random access memory.

Stack – first in, last out data structure. Can be hardware or software.

Stack pointer – a reference pointer to the top of the stack.

State machine – model of sequential processes.

Synchronous – using the same clock to coordinate operations.

System – a collection of interacting elements and relationships with a specific behavior.

Test-and-set – coordination mechanism for multiple processes that allows reading to a location and writing it in a non-interruptible manner.

TCP/IP – transmission control protocol/internet protocol; layered set of protocols for networks.

TMR – Triple Modular Redundancy; an error control mechanism using redundant components.

Transceiver – receiver and transmitter in one box.

TRAP – exception or fault handling mechanism in a computer; an operating system component.

Triplicate – using three copies (of hardware, software, messaging, power supplies, etc.). for redundancy and error control.

Tri-state – logic device with 2 state, plus a high-impedance state.

Truncate – discard. Cutoff, make shorter.

TTL – transistor-transistor logic in digital integrated circuits. (1963)

UART – universal asynchronous receiver-transmitter. Parallel-to-serial; serial-to parallel device with handshaking.

USART – universal synchronous (or) asynchronous receiver/transmitter.

Underflow – the result of an arithmetic operation is smaller than the smallest representable number.

USAF – United States Air Force.

Unsigned number – a number without a numeric sign.

Vector – single dimensional array of values.

VHDL- very high level description language; a language to describe integrated circuits and asic/ fpga's.

Via – vertical conducting pathway through an insulating layer in a semiconductor.

Von Neumann, John, a computer pioneer and mathematician; realized that computer instructions are data.

Watchdog – hardware/software function to sanity check the hardware, software, and process; applies corrective action if a fault is detected; fail-safe mechanism.

Wiki – the Hawaiian word for "quick." Refers to a collaborative content website.

Word – a collection of bits of any size; does not have to be a power of two.

Write-only – of no interest.

XOR – exclusive OR; either but not both.

Zener – voltage reference diode.

Zero address – architecture using implicit addressing, like a stack.

Bibliography

General, 16-bit

Coone, Jerome T. "An Implementation Guide to a Proposed Standard for Floating-Point Arithmetic," IEEE Computer, January 1980.

Dolhoff, Terry 16-bit *Microprocessor Architecture,* Brady, February 1980, ISBN 0835970019.

Osborne, Adam, Osborne *16-bit microprocessor Handbook,* Osborne/McGraw-Hill, 1981, ISBN 0931988438.

Rafiquzzaman, Mohamed, *Microprocessors: Theory and Applications* (Intel and Motorola), Prentice Hall, 1992, ISBN 0135881463.

Stakem, Patrick H. *8-bit Microprocessors,* 2013, PRB Publishing, ASIN - tbd.

Stakem, Patrick H. *Microprocessors in Space,* 2011, PRRB Publishing, ASIN B0057PFJQI.

Tracton, Ken *How to Build your own Working 16-bit Microcomputer,* Tab Books; 1st edition, 1979, ISBN-0830610995.

Triebel, Walter A. *16-bit Microprocessors: Architecture, Software, and Interface Techniques,* Prentice-Hall, 1985, ISBN 0138114072.

Triebel, Walter A. and Singh, Avtar *The 8088 and 8086 Microprocessors: Programming, Interfacing, Software, Hardware, and Applications* (4th Edition) 2002, Prentice Hall, ISBN 0130930814.

Wagner, T. J. Fundamentals of Microcomputer Programming Macmillan, 1984, ISBN 0024237108.

wikipedia, various.

Apollo AGC

The Apollo Flight Journal, The Apollo On-board Computers, http://history.nasa.gov/afj/compessay.htm

Apollo Guidance Computer emulator, http://www.ibiblio.org/apollo/index.html

Hall, Eldon C. *Journey to the Moon: The History of the Apollo Guidance Computer*, 1996, AIAA Press, ISBN 1-56347-185-X.

O'Brien, Frank *The Apollo Guidance Computer: Architecture and Operation*, Springer Praxis Books, 1st Edition, 2010, ISBN- 1441908765

DEC LSI-11

Desautels, E. J. *Understanding Computing using PDP-11 and LSI-11 Computers: Introduction to Computer Organization and Assembly Language Programming*, 1981 ASIN: B0006YJLL4.

1750A

http://legacy.cleanscape.net/stdprod/xtc1750a/resources/index.html

http://sd-www.jhuapl.edu/MSX/fact/MIL-STD-1750AAV.pdf

http://www.everyspec.com/MIL-STD/MIL-STD+%281700+-+1799%29/

Bit Slice

Kane, Adam and Osborne, Gerry. *Osborne's 16-bit Microprocessor Handbook, includes 2900 Chip Slice Family*, Osborne/McGraw-Hill (1981) ASIN: B00126NGL6.

Motorola 68000

Antonakos, James L. *The 68000 Microprocessor*, 5th ed, Prentice Hall; December 5, 2003, ISBN 0130195618.

Clements, Alan *Microprocessor Systems Design: 68000 Family Hardware, Software, and Interfacing*, CL-Engineering; 3rd ed. March 21, 1997, ISBN 0534948227.

Clements, Alan *68000 Family Assembly Language Programming*, CL Engineering; 1st ed, September 24, 1993) ISBN-0534932754.

Triebel, Walter A., Singh, Avtar *The 68000/68020 Microprocessors: Architecture, Software and Interfacing Techniques*, Prentice Hall; 1st edition, 1991, ISBN-013812132X.

MacKenzie, I. Scott *68000 Microprocessor*, Prentice Hall, 1995, ISBN-1 0023736542.

Wakerly, John F. *Microcomputer Architecture and Programming: The 68000 Family*, Wiley, 1st edition, January 1989, ISBN-0471853194.

Wilcox, Alan D. 68000 *Microcomputer Systems: Designing and Troubleshooting*, Prentice Hall, 1987, ISBN-0138114641.

M68000 *16/32 bit-Microprocessor: Programmer's Reference Manual*, Prentice-Hall; 4th edition, 1984, ISBN- 013566795X.

SoC

Davies, John H. *MSP430 Microcontroller Basics*, Newnes; 1st ed, 2008, ISBN- 0750682760.

Zengin, Salih *System-C Implementation of a RISC-Based Processor Architecture: Design and Implementation of a 16-bit RISC-based Processor Architecture with System-C Language*, VDM Verlag, March 22, 2009, ISBN-3639130359.

Intel X86

Agarwal, Rakesh K. *80X86 Architecture and Programming: Architecture Reference: Covers Implementations from the 8086 to the i486, and Includes the 80X87 Processor,* Prentice Hall, 1991, ISBN-10: 0132454327.

Antonakos, James L. *Introduction to the Intel Family of Microprocessors: A Hands-On Approach Utilizing the 80x86 Microprocessor Family*, (3rd Edition), Prentice Hall; 3rd edition, 1998, ISBN-10: 0138934398.

Gorsline, George W. *16-Bit Modern Microcomputers: The Intel i8086 Family,* Prentice Hall, 1985, ISBN-0138114153.

Goody, Roy W. *The 16-Bit Microprocessor: An 8086-8088 Based Product-Development Approach: Includes a*

Comparison of the iapx86, 186, 286, and 386 Families, Comptech Pub. Co., 1986, ISBN-0935397000.

Hummel, Robert L. *Programmer's Technical Reference: the Processor and co-processor,* 1992, Ziff-Davis, ISBN 1-56276-016-5.

Intel, Intel *80286 and 80287 Programmer's Reference Manual,* 1987, 210498.

Intel, *iAPX 286 Hardware Reference Manual,* Intel, 1983, 210760-001.

Intel, *80286 Operating Systems Writer's Guide,* 121960.

Intel, iAPX <u>86/88, 186/188 User's Manual, Programmer's Reference</u>, 1986, 210911-003.

Intel, iAPX *86/88, 186/188 User's Manual,* Hardware Reference, 1986, 210912-001.

Intel, *Embedded Controller Handbook,* (80186, 80188), 1987, 210918.

Intel, *Microprocessor and Peripheral Handbook,* 2 Vol., 1987, 230843.

Intel, *80130 Operating system Processor,* 1981, 210216-002.

Jackson, Tim *Inside Intel,* 1997, Plume, ISBN 0-525-94141-X.

Leinecker, Richard C. "Processor-Detection Schemes," Dr. Dobb's Journal, 1993 v18 i6 p46.

Morse, Stephan and Albert, Douglas *The 80286 Architecture*, Wiley Books, 1986, ISBN 0 471-83185-9.

Rash, Bill "iAPX 286 Loadall Instruction," Intel Technical Memo, November 21, 1984.

Scanlon, Leo J. 8086/8088/80286 Assembly Language, (Revised Edition), Brady Books,1988, ISBN 0-13-246919-7.

Scanlon, Leo, *8086/8088 Assembly Language Programming*, Brady Books, 1984, ISBN 0-89303-424-X.

Shanley, Tom *Protected Mode Software Architecture*, Addison-Wesley Professional, 1996, ISBN-020155447X.

Stakem, Patrick H. *Computer Architecture & Programming of the Intel x86 Family*, 2012, PRRB Publishing, ASIN B0078Q39D4.

Theis, Klaus-Dieter *The Innovative 80X86 Architectures: The 80286 Microprocessor*, Prentice Hall, 1991, ISBN-10: 0134672836.

Uffenbeck, John *The 80x86 Family: Design, Programming, and Interfacing* (3rd Edition) Prentice

Hall; 3 edition (February 14, 2001), ISBN-10: 0130257117.

Understanding X86 Microprocessors: 99 Articles Originally Published in Microprocessor Report Between September 1987 and April 1993, Ziff Davis Press, 1993, ISBN- 1562761587.

Wilt, Nicholas "Assembly Language Programming for the 80x87," Dr. Dobb's Journal 1992 v 17 i3 P. 36.

PIC

Lucio Di Jasio *Programming 16-Bit PIC Microcontrollers in C, Second Edition: Learning to Fly the PIC 24*, Newnes; 2 edition (December 28, 2011) ISBN-1856178706.

TMS-9900

Tesas Instruments, *TMS 9900 Microprocessor Data Manual*, December 1976, ASIN B0040LN0DO.

Tesas Instruments, *9900 Family Systems Design and Data Book* (Microprocessor series), 1st edition,1978, ISBN- 0895120267.

Zilog

Coffron, James *Using and Troubleshooting the Z8000*, Reston Pub. Co, 1982, ISBN- 0835981576.

Moore, Martin L. *Z8000 Handbook,* Prentice Hall; 1st Ed, 1982, ISBN- 013983866X.

Osborne, Adam, *Z8000 Assembly Language Programming*, Osborne/McGraw-Hill, 1980, ISBN-0079310362.

Computer Architecture, General

Augarten, Stan, *State of the Art,* 1983, Ticknor & Fields, ISBN 0-89919-206-8.

Bell, C. Gordon and Newell, Allen, *Computer Structures: Readings and Examples*, McGraw Hill Inc., January 1, 1971, ISBN- 0070043574.

Blaauw, Gerrit A. and Brooks, Frederick P. Jr. *Computer Architecture, Concepts and Evolution*, 2 volumes, 1997, Addison-Wesley, IBN 0-201-10557-8.

Bryant, Randal E., O'Hallaron, David R. *Computer systems: A Programmer's Perspective*, 2nd edition, Addison Wesley, Kindle e-book edition, ASIN: B004S81RXE.

Boole, George *An Investigation of the Laws of Thought on which are Founded the Mathematical Theories of Logic and Probability*, 1854, reprinted 1958, Dover, ISBN 0-48660028-9.

Burks, Arthur; W. Goldstein, Herman H.; Von Neumann, John "Preliminary Discussion of the Logical Design of an Electronic Computing Instrument," 1987, MIT Press, originally published in Papers of John Von Neumann on Computing and Computer Theory.

Carter, Nick Schaum's *Outline of Computer Architecture*, McGraw-Hill; 1st edition (December 26, 2001) ISBN-007136207X.

Comer, Douglas E. *Essentials of Computer Architecture,* Prentice Hall; US Ed edition (August 23, 2004) ISBN 0131491792.

Englander, Irv *The Architecture of Computer Hardware and Systems Software: An Information Technology Approach*, Wiley; 3 edition (January 20, 2003) ISBN-0471073253.

Flores, Ivan *The Logic of Computer Arithmetic*, 1963, Prentice-Hall, ISBN 0135400392.

Harris, David and Harris, Sarah *Digital Design and Computer Architecture,* Morgan Kaufmann (March 2, 2007) ISBN 012370497.9

Hennessy, John L. and Patterson, David A. *Computer Architecture, Fifth Edition: A Quantitative Approach,*

Morgan Kaufmann; (September 30, 2011) ISBN 012383872X.

Heuring, Vincent, and Jordan, Harry F. *Computer Systems Design and Architecture* (2nd Edition), Prentice Hall; 2 edition (December 6, 2003) ISBN 0130484407.

IEEE Computer *ANSI/IEEE Standard 754-1985 for Binary Floating-Point Arithmetic*, IEEE Computer, Jan. 1980.

Kidder, Tracy *The Soul of a New Machine*, Back Bay Books (June 2000) ISBN 0316491977.

Mano, M. Morris *Computer System Architecture* (3rd Edition), Prentice Hall; 3rd edition (October 29, 1992) ISBN 0131755633.

Murdocca, Miles J. and Heuring, Vincent Computer *Architecture and Organization: An Integrated Approach,* Wiley (March 16, 2007) ISBN 0471733881.

Nisan, Noam and Schocken, Shimon, *The Elements of Computing Systems: Building a Modern Computer from First Principles*, 2005, MIT Press, ISBN 0262640686.

Null, Linda *The Essentials of Computer Organization And Architecture*, Jones & Bartlett Pub; 2 edition (February 15, 2006) ISBN 0763737690.

Page, Daniel, *A Practical Introduction to Computer Architecture*, 2009, Springer, ISBN 1848822553.

Patterson, David A and Hennessy, John L. Computer *Organization and Design: The Hardware/Software Interface*, Revised Fourth Edition, Morgan Kaufmann; Nov. 2011 ISBN 0123744938.

Ramachandran, Umakishore, and Leahy, William D. Jr., *Computer Systems: An Integrated Approach to Architecture and Operating Systems,* 2010, Addison Wesley, ISBN 0321486137.

Reid, T. R. *The Chip: How Two Americans Invented the Microchip and Launched a Revolution,* Random House Trade Paperbacks; Revised edition (October 9, 2001) ISBN 0375758283.

Richards, R. K. *Arithmetic Operations in Digital Computers,* 1955, Van Nostrand, B00128Z00.

Schmid, Hermann *Decimal Computation*, 1974, Wiley, ISBN 0-471-76180-X.

Shriver, Bruce D. *The Anatomy of a High-Performance Microprocessor: A Systems Perspective,* Wiley-IEEE Computer Society Press (June 4, 1998) ISBN 0818684003.

Silc, Jurji, Robic, Borut, Ungerer, Theo *Processor Architecture: from Dataflow to Superscalar and Beyond,* Springer; 1st edition (July 20, 1999) ISBN 3540647988.

Slater, Michael *Microprocessor-Based Design A Comprehensive Guide to Effective Hardware Design,* 1989, Prentice Hall, ISBN 0-13-582248-3.

Stakem, Patrick H. *A Practitioner's Guide to RISC Microprocessor Architecture*, Wiley-Interscience, April 12, 1996, ISBN 0471130184.

Stallings, William *Computer Organization and Architecture: Designing for Performance* (7th Edition), Prentice Hall; 7 edition (July 21, 2005) ISBN 0131856448.

Stokes, Jon, *Inside the Machine An Illustrated Introduction to Microprocessors and Computer Architecture*, 2006, No Starch Press, ISBN 1593271042.

CADC

http://firstmicroprocessor.com/documents/ap1-26-97.pdf

Holt, Raymond M. *MOS Processor for the F14A CADC*, April 1971, Garrett AiResearch Corp., Technical Report 71-7266.

Holt, Ray M. F-14 "Tomcat" Microprocessor Chip Set, presentation, 1998. www.firstmicroprocessor.com.

Resources

http://www.ibm.com/developerworks/library/pa-microhist.html

http://www.intel.com/content/www/us/en/company-overview/intel-museum.html

www.antiquetech.com

www.CPU-world.com

www.CPUshack.com

www.happytrees.org/chips CPU graveyard

http://landley.net/history/mirror/tech/processors/CPU.html#tableofcontents

http://www.ibm.com/developerworks/library/pa-microhist.html.

http://klabs.org/

http://www.CPU-collection.de

www.bitsavers.org

http://www.s100computers.com/History.htm "A Short History of Microprocessors" http://datasheets.chipdb.org/

16-bit Microprocessors, CPU Museum of Japan,
http://www.shmj.or.jp/english/pdf/ic/exhibi748E.pdf

1970's Development and Evolution of Microprocessors,
Seemiconductor Museum of Japan.

https://web.archive.org/web/20190627161417/http://www
w.shmj.or.jp/english/pdf/ic/exhibi748E.pdf

If you enjoyed this book, you might also be interested in some of these.

Stakem, Patrick H. *16-bit Microprocessors, History and Architecture*, 2013 PRRB Publishing, ISBN-1520210922.

Stakem, Patrick H. *4- and 8-bit Microprocessors, Architecture and History*, 2013, PRRB Publishing, ISBN-152021572X,

Stakem, Patrick H. *Apollo's Computers,* 2014, PRRB Publishing, ISBN-1520215800.

Stakem, Patrick H. *The Architecture and Applications of the ARM Microprocessors,* 2013, PRRB Publishing, ISBN-1520215843.

Stakem, Patrick H. *Earth Rovers: for Exploration and Environmental Monitoring,* 2014, PRRB Publishing, ISBN-152021586X.

Stakem, Patrick H. *Embedded Computer Systems, Volume 1, Introduction and Architecture*, 2013, PRRB Publishing, ISBN-1520215959.

Stakem, Patrick H. *The History of Spacecraft Computers from the V-2 to the Space Station*, 2013, PRRB Publishing, ISBN-1520216181.

Stakem, Patrick H. *Floating Point Computation*, 2013, PRRB Publishing, ISBN-152021619X.

Stakem, Patrick H. *Architecture of Massively Parallel Microprocessor Systems*, 2011, PRRB Publishing, ISBN-1520250061.

Stakem, Patrick H. *Multicore Computer Architecture,* 2014, PRRB Publishing, ISBN-1520241372.

Stakem, Patrick H. *Personal Robots*, 2014, PRRB Publishing, ISBN-1520216254.

Stakem, Patrick H. *RISC Microprocessors, History and Overview,* 2013, PRRB Publishing, ISBN-1520216289.

Stakem, Patrick H. *Robots and Telerobots in Space Applications*, 2011, PRRB Publishing, ISBN-1520210361.

Stakem, Patrick H. *The Saturn Rocket and the Pegasus Missions, 1965,* 2013, PRRB Publishing, ISBN-1520209916.

Stakem, Patrick H. *Visiting the NASA Centers, and Locations of Historic Rockets & Spacecraft,* 2017, PRRB Publishing, ISBN-1549651205.

Stakem, Patrick H. *Microprocessors in Space*, 2011, PRRB Publishing, ISBN-1520216343.

Stakem, Patrick H. *Computer Virtualization and the Cloud*, 2013, PRRB Publishing, ISBN-152021636X.

Stakem, Patrick H. *What's the Worst That Could Happen? Bad Assumptions, Ignorance, Failures and Screw-ups in Engineering Projects, 2014,* PRRB Publishing, ISBN-1520207166.

Stakem, Patrick H. *Computer Architecture & Programming of the Intel x86 Family, 2013,* PRRB Publishing, ISBN-1520263724.

Stakem, Patrick H. *The Hardware and Software Architecture of the Transputer*, 2011,PRRB Publishing, ISBN-152020681X.

Stakem, Patrick H. *Mainframes, Computing on Big Iron*, 2015, PRRB Publishing, ISBN- 1520216459.

Stakem, Patrick H. *Spacecraft Control Centers*, 2015, PRRB Publishing, ISBN-1520200617.

Stakem, Patrick H. *Embedded in Space,* 2015, PRRB Publishing, ISBN-1520215916.

Stakem, Patrick H. *A Practitioner's Guide to RISC Microprocessor Architecture*, Wiley-Interscience, 1996, ISBN-0471130184.

Stakem, Patrick H. *Cubesat Engineering*, PRRB Publishing, 2017, ISBN-1520754019.

Stakem, Patrick H. *Cubesat Operations*, PRRB Publishing, 2017, ISBN-152076717X.

Stakem, Patrick H. *Interplanetary Cubesats*, PRRB Publishing, 2017, ISBN-1520766173 .

Stakem, Patrick H. Cubesat Constellations, Clusters, and Swarms, Stakem, PRRB Publishing, 2017, ISBN-1520767544.

Stakem, Patrick H. *Graphics Processing Units, an overview*, 2017, PRRB Publishing, ISBN-1520879695.

Stakem, Patrick H. *Intel Embedded and the Arduino-101, 2017,* PRRB Publishing, ISBN-1520879296.

Stakem, Patrick H. *Orbital Debris, the problem and the mitigation*, 2018, PRRB Publishing, ISBN-*1980466483.*

Stakem, Patrick H. *Manufacturing in Space*, 2018, PRRB Publishing, ISBN-1977076041.

Stakem, Patrick H. *NASA's Ships and Planes*, 2018, PRRB Publishing, ISBN-1977076823.

Stakem, Patrick H. *Space Tourism*, 2018, PRRB Publishing, ISBN-1977073506.

Stakem, Patrick H. *STEM – Data Storage and Communications*, 2018, PRRB Publishing, ISBN-1977073115.

Stakem, Patrick H. *In-Space Robotic Repair and Servicing*, 2018, PRRB Publishing, ISBN-1980478236.

Stakem, Patrick H. *Introducing Weather in the pre-K to 12 Curricula, A Resource Guide for Educators*, 2017, PRRB Publishing, ISBN-1980638241.

Stakem, Patrick H. *Introducing Astronomy in the pre-K to 12 Curricula, A Resource Guide for Educators*, 2017, PRRB Publishing, ISBN-198104065X.

Also available in a Brazilian Portuguese edition, ISBN-1983106127.

Stakem, Patrick H. *Deep Space Gateways, the Moon and Beyond*, 2017, PRRB Publishing, ISBN-1973465701.

Stakem, Patrick H. *Exploration of the Gas Giants, Space Missions to Jupiter, Saturn, Uranus, and Neptune*, PRRB Publishing, 2018, ISBN-9781717814500.

Stakem, Patrick H. *Crewed Spacecraft*, 2017, PRRB Publishing, ISBN-1549992406.

Stakem, Patrick H. *Rocketplanes to Space*, 2017, PRRB Publishing, ISBN-1549992589.

Stakem, Patrick H. *Crewed Space Stations,* 2017, PRRB Publishing, ISBN-1549992228.

Stakem, Patrick H. *Enviro-bots for STEM: Using Robotics in the pre-K to 12 Curricula, A Resource Guide for Educators,* 2017, PRRB Publishing, ISBN-1549656619.

Stakem, Patrick H. *STEM-Sat, Using Cubesats in the pre-K to 12 Curricula, A Resource Guide for Educators*, 2017, ISBN-1549656376.

Stakem, Patrick H. *Lunar Orbital Platform-Gateway*, 2018, PRRB Publishing, ISBN-1980498628.

Stakem, Patrick H. *Embedded GPU's*, 2018, PRRB Publishing, ISBN- 1980476497.

Stakem, Patrick H. *Mobile Cloud Robotics*, 2018, PRRB Publishing, ISBN- 1980488088.

Stakem, Patrick H. *Extreme Environment Embedded Systems,* 2017, PRRB Publishing, ISBN-1520215967.

Stakem, Patrick H. *What's the Worst, Volume-2*, 2018, ISBN-1981005579.

Stakem, Patrick H., *Spaceports*, 2018, ISBN-1981022287.

Stakem, Patrick H., *Space Launch Vehicles*, 2018, ISBN-1983071773.

Stakem, Patrick H. *Mars*, 2018, ISBN-1983116902.

Stakem, Patrick H. *X-86, 40th Anniversary ed*, 2018, ISBN-1983189405.

Stakem, Patrick H. *Lunar Orbital Platform-Gateway*, 2018, PRRB Publishing, ISBN-1980498628.

Stakem, Patrick H. *Space Weather*, 2018, ISBN-1723904023.

Stakem, Patrick H. *STEM-Engineering Process*, 2017, ISBN-1983196517.

Stakem, Patrick H. *Space Telescopes,* 2018, PRRB Publishing, ISBN-1728728568.

Stakem, Patrick H. *Exoplanets*, 2018, PRRB Publishing, ISBN-9781731385055.

Stakem, Patrick H. *Planetary Defense*, 2018, PRRB Publishing, ISBN-9781731001207.

Patrick H. Stakem *Exploration of the Asteroid Belt*, 2018, PRRB Publishing, ISBN-1731049846.

Patrick H. Stakem *Terraforming*, 2018, PRRB Publishing, ISBN-1790308100.

Patrick H. Stakem, *Martian Railroad,* 2019, PRRB Publishing, ISBN-1794488243.

Patrick H. Stakem, *Exoplanets,* 2019, PRRB Publishing, ISBN-1731385056.

Patrick H. Stakem, *Exploiting the Moon,* 2019, PRRB Publishing, ISBN-1091057850.

Patrick H. Stakem, *RISC-V, an Open Source Solution for Space Flight Computers,* 2019, PRRB Publishing, ISBN-1796434388.

Patrick H. Stakem, *Arm in Space*, 2019, PRRB Publishing, ISBN-9781099789137.

Patrick H. Stakem, *Extraterrestrial Life*, 2019, PRRB Publishing, ISBN-978-1072072188.

Patrick H. Stakem, *Space Command*, 2019, PRRB Publishing, ISBN-978-1693005398.

CubeRovers, A Synergy of Technologys, 2020, PRRB Publishing, ISBN-979-8651773138.

Robotic Exploration of the Icy moons of the Gas Giants. 2020, PRRB Publishing, ISBN- 979-8621431006

Hacking Cubesats, 2020, PRRB Publishing, ISBN-979-8623458964.

History & Future of Cubesats, PRRB Publishing, ISBN-979-8649179386.

Hacking Cubesats, Cybersecurity in Space, 2020, PRRB Publishing, ISBN-979-8623458964.

Powerships, Powerbarges, Floating Wind Farms: electricity when and where you need it, 2021, PRRB Publishing, ISBN-979-8716199477.

Hospital Ships, Trains, and Aircraft, 2020, PRRB Publishing, ISBN-979-8642944349.

2020/2021 Releases

CubeRovers, a Synergy of Technologys, 2020, ISBN-979-8651773138

Exploration of Lunar & Martian Lava Tubes by Cube-X, ISBN-979-8621435325.

History & Future of Cubesats, ISBN-978-1986536356.

Robotic Exploration of the Icy Moons of the Ice Giants, by Swarms of Cubesats, ISBN-979-8621431006.

Swarm Robotics, ISBN-979-8534505948.

Introduction to Electric Power Systems, ISBN-979-8519208727.

Centros de Control: Operaciones en Satélites del Estándar CubeSat (Spanish Edition), 2021, ISBN-979-8510113068.

Exploration of Venus, 2022, ISBN-979-8484416110.

Patrick H. Stakem, *The Search for Extraterrestial Life,* 2019, PRRB Publishing, ISBN-1072072181.

The Artemis Missions, Return to the Moon, and on to Mars, 2021, ISBN-979-8490532361.

James Webb Space Telescope. A New Era in Astronomy, 2021, ISBN-979-8773857969.

www.ingramcontent.com/pod-product-compliance
Lightning Source LLC
Chambersburg PA
CBHW031226050326
40689CB00009B/1490